MIRACLE
IN THE
MORNING

The Wonderful Story of Easter

MARY E. ERICKSON
Illustrated by JENNY WILLIAMS

Faith
KiDs

Equipping Kids
for Life

Chariot Books™ is an imprint of Chariot Family Publishing
Cook Communications, Colorado Springs, CO 80918
Cook Communications, Paris, Ontario
Kingsway Communications, Eastbourne, England

MIRACLE IN THE MORNING: THE WONDERFUL STORY OF EASTER
©1994 by Mary Erickson for text and Jenny Williams for illustrations

Scripture quotation is from the Holy Bible, New International Version, ©1973, 1978, 1984, International Bible Society. Used by permission of Zondervan Bible Publishers.

Designed by Bob Fuller Creative

First Printing, 1994
Printed in China
99 98 97 96 95 6 5 4 3 2

Library of Congress Cataloging-in-Publication Data
Erickson, Mary E.
Miracle in the morning: the wonderful story of Easter/by Mary E. Erickson.
        p.   cm.
Summary: Describes the final days, crucifixion, and resurrection of Jesus Christ.
ISBN 0-7814-0779-6
1. Jesus Christ—Resurrection—Juvenile literature. 2. Bible stories, English—N.T. Gospels. [1. Jesus Christ—Resurrection. 2. Bible stories—N.T.] I. Title.
BT481.E75 1993
232.9'7—dc20   92-20260
                                                                      CIP
                                                                      AC

For God so loved the world
that he gave his one and only Son,
that whoever believes in him
shall not perish but have eternal life.

John 3:16

Jerusalem was crowded on a Sunday afternoon. Suddenly a shout went up. "Here comes our King!" a messenger cried.

A procession came through the city gates. At the front of the line were children. Next came Jesus, riding on a young donkey. Cheering crowds came behind.

Men laid their cloaks in the road for Jesus to ride over. Women waved palm branches. Children sang, "Hosanna! Hosanna! Jesus is our King!"

Three men in temple robes watched from a rooftop.

"The whole world is following Jesus," said a man with a gruff voice.

Another man frowned. "He will soon be their leader instead of us. We must get rid of Him."

"I have a plan," said the third man. "Let's tell lies about Him." He sneered. "We'll change this cheering crowd into an angry mob before the week is over."

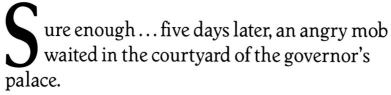

S ure enough ... five days later, an angry mob waited in the courtyard of the governor's palace.

Soon Governor Pilate appeared on the palace porch. Behind him stood Jesus, wearing a crown of thorns and a purple robe.

Pilate asked the crowd, "What shall I do with Jesus, King of the Jews?"

"He is not our king!" the people shouted. "Crucify Him! Crucify Him!"

Soldiers laid a heavy cross upon Jesus' shoulder. Slowly He dragged it down the stone steps of the city streets.

Scr-ape! Thud! Scr-ape! Thud!

The sound echoed in the narrow passageways of Jerusalem.

Mary, Jesus' mother, wept as she followed her son. Several friends walked beside her.

Mary Magdalene put her arm around Mary. "Jesus is good and kind," she said. "I'll always remember how He healed me."

Salome cried out, "He did nothing wrong! Why are they treating Him like this?"

Jesus struggled beneath the heavy cross. He stumbled and fell.

Then a stranger stepped out of the crowd. He lifted the cross and carried it up the hill called Calvary.

Roman soldiers nailed the hands and feet of Jesus to the wooden cross. Then they raised it between the crosses of two robbers.

At noon, storm clouds hung low in the sky. The sun disappeared. Thunder rolled and rumbled overhead. Frightened people shivered in the darkness.

At three o'clock, fierce winds bent the trees. The earth shook. Rocks split and tumbled down the hill. Screaming people ran for shelter.

The women who loved Jesus huddled near the cross.

"Listen," said Mary Magdalene. "Jesus is speaking."

"Heavenly Father," Jesus prayed. "My work is finished. Take my spirit to heaven to be with You." Jesus bowed His head and died.

Two friends, Joseph of Arimathea and Nicodemus, lifted Jesus' body down from the cross. They carried His body to a nearby garden. The women followed.

Jesus' friends washed away the dried blood from His hands and feet. They rubbed His body with olive oil and wrapped Him in strips of soft white cloth.

Wiping away her tears, Mary Magdalene said, "It's too late to bury His body properly tonight."

One of the other women nodded. "After the sabbath day is past, we can return with spices and perfumes."

The women watched as Joseph and Nicodemus carried the body of Jesus into the tomb carved in the hillside.

Inside it was dark and hollow like a cave. The air was damp and musty. The men laid Jesus' body on a cold stone shelf. Sadly they left the tomb.

Grunting and straining, the two men rolled a huge stone in front of the entrance.

With heads lowered, everyone left the garden.

Later some soldiers marched into the garden. Holding shields and spears, they stood stiff and straight in front of the sealed tomb.

"Why are we here, anyway?" grumbled one.

"To guard the tomb," his captain snapped. "Jesus' followers might try to steal His body and pretend He came back to life."

During the night, a great earthquake shook the ground.

"Look!" One of the soldiers pointed to a strange light in the dark night.

Down from heaven came an angel, surrounded with dazzling light. His face shone as he rolled away the stone. Then he sat upon it.

The captain fainted. The guards fainted.

When they awoke, the angel was gone.

Carrying lanterns, two soldiers searched the tomb.

"It's empty!" one exclaimed. "The body is gone."

"Woe is me," the captain groaned. "No one will believe us. But we must hurry to the city and report what happened."

At dawn on Sunday morning, four women returned to the garden.

Mary Magdalene carried a wooden box. "I mixed some sweet-smelling spices for the body of our Lord," she said.

"And I brought perfume to sprinkle over the white cloths." Salome hugged a vase close to her heart.

"I'm worried," another Mary told Joanna as they followed a path through a grove of olive trees. "How will we ever roll back the stone by ourselves?"

They passed rows of tiny purple flowers opening their petals to the morning sun.

"Oh!" Joanna caught her breath. "The stone! Someone has moved the stone!"

Mary Magdalene rushed to the tomb and looked inside. "Jesus is gone!" she cried. "I must tell Peter and John!"

Dropping her box of spices, she ran down the path, leaving the others behind.

Inside the tomb, Salome, Joanna, and the other Mary stood weeping. The rising sun sent a narrow sunbeam across the empty stone shelf.

Salome whispered, "I wonder who took Jesus away."

Suddenly swishing sounds filled the air. A dazzling light filled the tomb.

The women covered their faces with their hands.

"Do not be afraid," an angel said. "I know you are looking for Jesus. He is not here. He has risen!"

A second angel spoke. "God raised Jesus from the dead. Go and find the disciples. Tell them Jesus is alive."

Then the angels disappeared.

Salome breathed deeply. "My heart is beating so fast."

"Mine, too," Joanna said. "But I don't know if it's from joy or fear."

Clapping her hands, Mary said, "Let's hurry. I can't wait to tell the others the good news."

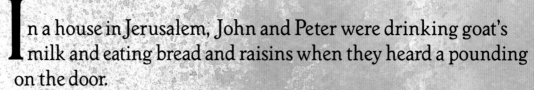

In a house in Jerusalem, John and Peter were drinking goat's milk and eating bread and raisins when they heard a pounding on the door.

Mary Magdalene burst into the room. "Jesus is gone!"

Peter and John raced to the garden.

John reached the tomb first, but he paused at the entrance. Peter pushed past John and rushed into the tomb.

"It's true!" Peter said. "He's gone. Do you think robbers stole His body?"

"Would robbers bother to undress the body and do that?" John pointed to the burial cloth neatly folded on the stone shelf.

With a puzzled expression, Peter rubbed his beard.

Like a gentle wave rolling over the beach, a peaceful feeling flooded over John. In his heart, he knew that Jesus had risen from the dead.

Outside the tomb John asked Mary Magdalene, "Will you return to the city with us?"

She shook her head. "I want to stay here alone for a while."

John and Peter hurried back to Jerusalem.

Alone in the garden, Mary Magdalene remembered happy times with Jesus. *He did so much for me, and I had so little time to be His helper.*

With tears in her eyes, she stooped and gazed into the tomb.

Two angels sat on the empty stone shelf.

One angel asked, "Woman, why are you crying?"

Mary answered, "They took away my Lord, and I don't know where they put Him."

With her head down, Mary turned away. She saw the robe and sandals of someone standing beside her.

"Why are you crying?" a kind voice asked.

Mary thought it was the gardener. "Sir, did you carry Jesus away? Please tell me where you put His body."

The voice spoke tenderly. "Mary."

Mary knew that voice. *How can it be?* she wondered.

But looking up, she saw the smiling face of Jesus. With joy she cried out, "My Lord! My Master! You're alive. You've risen from the dead."

She knelt at His feet to worship Him.

The other three women were hurrying to Jerusalem. Thorny plants with yellow petals lined the road. Wild flowers colored the hillside.

Salome asked Joanna and Mary, "Do you believe what the angels told us—that we'll see Jesus?"

But before anyone could answer, Jesus appeared in the road ahead. "Good morning!" He said.

"Master, is it really You?" Salome's voice quivered.

"Don't be frightened," Jesus said. "Be filled with joy!"

Kneeling in the road, the women worshiped Him.

"Get up," said Jesus, "and go tell My disciples that I am alive."

Then He disappeared.

"This is a wonderful day!" Salome danced in the road. "I feel like singing. Jesus was dead, but now He's alive."

"Yes!" said Joanna. "It's just like springtime. Trees are sprouting leaves. Flowers are blooming. Baby animals are making soft sounds."

"Baa-baa! Baa-baa!" Woolly lambs nibbled new grass.

"Peep! Peep!" Fuzzy chicks scratched the dirt.

"Thank You, God," prayed Mary, "for this very special spring."

On Sunday evening, ten of the disciples were eating supper together.

Andrew asked, "Do you believe the women *really* saw Jesus?"

"Maybe it was a dream," Philip suggested.

Suddenly Jesus appeared in the locked room. "Peace be with you!" He said.

Philip's mouth fell open. "It's a ghost!"

"Why do you doubt?" Jesus reached out both His hands. "Touch Me. Does a ghost have a body?"

Jesus joined them at the table. He ate a bite of broiled fish. He dipped a biscuit into honey butter. While His disciples watched, Jesus chewed and swallowed the food.

Andrew cried out, "I believe it's You, Lord!"

"Me, too," said Philip, "but what does it mean? Why did You die?"

"It was written in God's plan," Jesus explained. "I died for you and for the world, to forgive your sins. I am your risen Savior. Whoever believes in Me will live with Me in heaven forever and ever."

The next Sunday the disciples met again. John said, "One week ago Jesus rose from the dead. He appeared to us here in this room. Let's praise God. Let's celebrate the resurrection of Jesus, our Lord."

"I wasn't here," Thomas said boldly, throwing out his hands. "I won't believe unless I see Jesus myself and put my finger in the nail holes in His hands."

Suddenly Jesus was there with them. "Peace be with you!" He said.

Thomas breathed louder and faster. His eyes opened wide.

Jesus stretched out His hands. "Touch Me, Thomas," He said. "Put your finger in the nail holes. Stop doubting and believe."

With trembling fingers, the doubting disciple touched the nail holes. Falling to his knees, he cried, "My Lord and my God!"

Jesus stroked his head. "Because you see Me, Thomas, you believe. Blessed are the people who believe I am the risen Savior even though they cannot see Me."

A few days later, in the early morning, seven tired disciples were hauling empty nets into Peter's fishing boat.

"Friends!" someone called from the shore of Lake Galilee. "Did you catch anything?"

"Nothing!" shouted Peter.

The stranger called back, "Cast your net into the lake once more—on the right side this time. You'll catch something."

The disciples tried again.

In a flash, the net was filled with flipping, flopping fish.

"Who is that man?" Peter wondered.

Suddenly John cried out, "It's Jesus!"

With a splash, Peter leaped into the lake and swam to shore. The other disciples rowed the boat, dragging the bulging net behind.

When they reached the shore, they saw Jesus tending a fire. Fish sizzled on the burning coals.

"Come and eat breakfast," He called.

Seven excited disciples sat on the sand.

Jesus served them bread and fish.

The eleven disciples traveled to a mountain in Galilee to meet Jesus. Many believers followed.

Children climbed over the rocks, picking ferns and flowers. Men and women talked about the resurrection.

"Look!" shouted a boy on a big rock. "Here comes Jesus!"

A little girl ran down the mountain to meet Him. Jesus reached down and swooped her up.

Anxious to hear Jesus speak, the crowd quickly gathered around Him.

"Soon I'm going to be with my heavenly Father," Jesus said. "After I'm gone, there's something important I want you to do."

"What is it?" asked a disciple. "We will gladly do it."

"Tell people in every land that I died to forgive their sins. I want people everywhere to believe in Me and become My disciples. Teach them to obey everything I have taught you."

"We promise," said another disciple.

"And here's a promise for you," Jesus said, "and to everyone who believes in Me. Wherever you go and whatever you do, I will always be with you."

Miracle in the Morning

Age: 4-7

Life Issue: I want my child to understand the true meaning of Easter and what it means to him or her today.

Spiritual Building Block: Easter/Faith

Learning Styles

Sight: Look for appropriate Easter sights for your child to see—a play at your church, the story of Easter on television, or a children's video presentation of the Easter story. Discuss why it was important for Jesus to die on the cross so that we can obtain salvation.

Sound: Look for a tape or CD that has a song about being in God's family. (The Gaither's have written a song called "The Family of God" that might work nicely.) Teach it to your child. Talk about the blessing of being a part of God's family.

Touch: Plan Easter activities with your child. Make a list of all the things you are going to do (hunt for eggs, go to church, have Easter dinner, etc.). Let him or her assist you in making something for this special day. Discuss the importance of having a plan. God had a plan to make us a part of His family. Explain that plan using the Easter story. Memorize John 3:16 together.

"For God so loved the world that he gave his one and only Son,
that whoever believes in him shall not perish but have eternal life."
John 3:16 (NIV)